ADIE *and* ALICE

Sisters with a Special Life

T. K. OWENS

Kravitz & Sons

INNOVATORS IN PUBLISHING, MARKETING AND ADVERTISING

Kravitz and Sons LLC
204 E Arlington Blvd. Suite B
Greenville, NC 27858

Published by Kravitz and Sons LLC.

ISBN: 979-8-89639-394-8 (sc)
ISBN: 979-8-89639-393-1 (e)

ADIE
and
ALICE

Sisters with a Special Life

T.K. OWENS

I turned my car into the parking lot of 'the home', and as usual, did not really want to get out and go inside. As I got paperwork together that needed to be handed out to staff, I also began to mentally brace myself to face the residents.

After 21 years in the nursing career, I've long ago given up on the idea of having all the answers. But most of the time I do like to feel in control. I was not feeling like the answer lady OR in much control of my world, at least the part where with Ellendale Home.

I walked in the side door of the building, trying to slip into the med station without being noticed. The building itself was started in 1956, with several additions. The floors are bumpy, the wiring conspicuously hidden around the top of the walls. Electric outlets are old and few.

"Hello, funny woman," Marie speaks with a muffled voice, somewhat like someone trying to speak with their teeth clinched. She came up to me quickly, holding her hands in front of her stomach, and turning her head to one side, looking up at the ceiling. We all knew her pose, the one that says, 'look at me'. This is my cue to tell her that her hair looks very nice. I then also need to remark on her flowered blouse.

"Oh, Marie, that is a very nice hair do, who did your hair today?" I asked as I shuffled papers.

"Karen, she braided my hair. Does it look nice?"

"Yes, it does.

Marie is 73 years, a thin woman who stands with her head cocked to one side. One eye that seems to forget it should look straight ahead. That is the one she usually turns away from you if she is trying to get your attention. She walks independently and can do most of her own care at this time. She faithfully makes her bed every morning. She likes to keep her room tidy. She must have learned this process while in a large institution for mentally retarded.

"I need more bras", hugging me her face closer to me as if it should be a secret between us. "Can you get me new bras?"

"Yes, I'll get you new bras, but not today."

"Okay, I like white," she smiles a lopsided smile and walked away.

Ruth came around the corner from the shower room. "Janet needs bras also," Ruth added to the list.

"What size do they wear?" I am reluctant to start a shopping list. I just want to be the nurse, the one they call with nursing issues. I have that 'feeling' starting in my stomach. I just know my role of 'the nurse' is going to become complicated.

"Big, trust me, big. I feel sorry for them each time I shower them. My grandmother was a buxom woman, and she had severe backaches and neck pain. I wonder if that is why Janet leans forward so much.

"I guess I'll be taking a shopping list with me. Can we work as a group, check the needs of everyone so I can make one trip?"

"You don't sound like you want to shop", Ruth looked at me as if I was a mutant female of some sort.

"Don't like to go shopping for clothing. Never have, not for myself or someone else. I don't mind spending money, I just don't like the sport of 'SHOPPING', making my point by raising my arms above my head like an Olympian.

"I never met a woman before who did not like to go shopping. Especially having free reign on what to buy, using other people's money!" Ruth actually had a squinted look, as trying to see some sort of deformity in me.

"Well, you have met one now." I started down the hallway to the chart room.

The hallway is clear, and I quickly look into each room as I walk by, just to check on the residents. One of my jobs is to be sure all the chart information is complete, because survey teams can visit us at any time. I've decided I want to have a system in place that will be easy to keep up with, and that I can hand parts of two other staff members.

Tom and I became owners of this residential care facility about two months before. The home was close to being closed, and I was asked to be an RN Consultant for the owner. Little by little, conversation here, meeting there and Voila, we were buying the business. I was trying to finish checking the charts of the new residents and made sure their TB tests were charted.

We were expecting the survey team to come back in any day, and I was feeling a push from behind to get the rest of the charts reviewed. I quietly shut the door to the chart room so I could have uninterrupted time to get this important paperwork done.

The door slowly opened, and Janet began to walk into the room.

"Can I ask you something?" she asked "Not right now, Janet. I am working. You know not to just open a door and walk in." I gently turned her around and nudged her over the threshold so I could shut the door again. But it didn't stay closed.

"I want to ask you something. Kerry hit me on the shoulder. She just hit me, and I wasn't doing nothing. Why did she do that? Unlike her sister's raspy whispered voice, Janets is clear and slurred. She is the older of the two, and very definitely the 'boss' of their relationship.

She stood in front of me, looking at me after her declaration. I knew I had no words of wisdom but if I didn't respond she would not go find something to do.

"I don't know why that happened" I responded.

"Hunh?"

"I wasn't there, I did not see what happened." I leaned closer to speak into her ear.

"I wasn't doing anything and Kelly just came up and hit me on the shoulder. Want to see where I was?" She pointed down the hall.

"No, I'll talk to Kelly later about this and tell her not to do it again. Okay?" I again turned her toward the doorway and escorted her out to the hall. As if it was time to be my rescuer, Mark came around the corner and took her hand, leading her away to the dining room.

Janet has no teeth; she is very unsteady on her feet because she leans forward almost 10 degrees. She began to tell Mark about her attack. I briefly watched them walking side by side. His figure tall, straight, a 25-year-old man leading Janet with skinny, hunched over with thick soled tennis shoes that made her thin legs look like stalks.

I went back to checking charts and enjoyed an hour of work time. This was what I wanted with this business venture. I wanted to come in, push some papers, evaluation systems, direct staff and leave. Most of all, I did not want to get close to the residents.

"Okay, how do we do this shopping thing?"

Carol is my best buddy, and so willing to help me shop for the residents. She works V2 days on Monday and agreed to help me with my 'huge' shopping task. I took her to breakfast and then we headed for the Goodwill Store with carte blanche.

"I have a list of who and what size. And we need to start looking at special things for Christmas presents too. I guess we just go up and down the aisles. I think we need to take two carts, we'll fill them". I was banking on Carol's good taste and the fact she had been with the residents at Ellendale a few times.

"I have a list of who and what size. And we need to start looking at special things for Christmas presents too. I guess we just go up and down the aisles. I think we need to take two carts, we'll fill them". I was banking on Carol's good taste and the fact she had been with the residents at Ellendale a few times.

For some reason, I looked at my watch as we started pushing the carts into the store. 10:15am, just after the store opened.

I looked at my watch again as the clerk at the cash register began to take items off the top of one cart. 12:20pm. 2 hours and 5 minutes to shop for 30 people I hardly know. I continually commented to Carol how wonderful she was to help me with this.

The clerk looked at both carts piled high with clothing. She looked at the other registers out of the corner of her eyes, her lips pursed together as if she was trying to decide whether to tackle this one by herself or call for back up.

"We are buying for about 30 people", I said. I realized I blurted this explanation out as if needing to explain the two carts piled so high we had to keep our hands on top of the pile to steady the loads.

Item by item, the three of us worked through over a hundred items of clothing. In a silent, woman-like style the three of us set up an assembly line. Carol took items out of the carts, handing them to the clerk with the tag visible. The clerk punched in the tag code and handed it to me to fold and put it in bags. In about 35 minutes we had reduced the 'raw items' into 25 plastic bags. Back in the two carts, we pushed them out of the van. Carol took the carts back to the front of the store and joined me, standing and looking at the pile of bags of clothes filling the back of the van.

"Something missing?" she asked "I hope not, after all that. I'm just trying to figure out how to process them when I get them back to the office."

"You're the system's expert; it will come to you. And since you do that systems thing so well, I'll bet your system is smooth as silk".

"Thanks for the confidence. I don't suppose you want to come out and help with that too?" I feigned a verbal jab.

"Nope, got to go home. This sparked my energy to do some shopping for myself," and she waved goodbye as I got in the van.

"This 'sparked' my energy to never go shopping again." I thought. The good news was that we'd got almost everything on the list. However, I had to wrap everything for Christmas.

I sat in the office conference room, looking at the 25 bags of clothing. Of the 23 people we shopped for, 13 of them have no family to help them with this or any other task. Some had outlived their parents and many brothers or sisters. Some had family members living in other care homes. A few are the last of their families still living. In Janet and Marie's case, they are the only family each other has. This seemed to rise to my awareness often as I did things for them or with them.

I had a lot of clothing and 'stuff' and I had a lot of plastic bags. I began the project of dividing up the purchases one resident at a time. Mary Ann, bras, shirts, socks, large teddy bear. Put all that in one bag, mark the name on the bag, put it aside for wrapping. I was 1/2 way through the process when Tom came into the office conference room.

He stood in the doorway, acting like he was not sure how safe it would be to enter the room. "What's all this?" He asked.

"I'm dividing up the stuff so we can wrap it", I didn't look up.

"Oh, okay. I'll just keep out of your way", and he went into his office.

By the time I was finished, I was surrounded by 30 bags of "Christmas" that would need to be wrapped within the next 3 weeks.

Christmas seemed to be a very important holiday for the residents. Those who had family near enough to come visit might go out somewhere, usually on a day during the week before Christmas. Those who did not have family near, or anywhere, seemed to look on Christmas as a time to get a present and sing songs. Marie and Janet knew Santa Claus would bring them things. And they knew how to get their order in to Santa Claus. They told staff members what they wanted.

In the weeks before Christmas Day, there were many chores to do, so the festive spirit filled the building. Decorations were put on the walls. The trees and deck in the courtyard were filled with flashing lights. Presents began to arrive by mail, and we did our best to intercept them. We'd sent out notices to all family to send presents to the home, not to the residents. That way we could hold them until Christmas day. This worked well, but the storage room in the office was getting stuffed by the 19th of December.

I started wrapping packages on Thursday, a week before Christmas. I did get a bit of help here and there, but my system seemed to be easy to follow only by me. When we spend money on clothing, presents, etc., we use the resident's PIF (Personal Incidental Fund). They get so much each month, and we must keep records of what was spent on what. Since I kept the PIF accounts, I had a great plan.

I would take one sack, and with a 5X8 card, remove the tags from each item for that resident, taping them on the card. The card, with the resident's name, was then set in a pile. Then I would wrap the presents and be sure that resident's name was on each gift. When all 25 bags had been reduced to some 65 packages, I then took the 5X8 cards and added that expense to their individual PIF ledgers.

I had this thought in my mind, needing to keep close track of what was spent, so that at some point someone would challenge my record keeping process. Each resident was given $70 a month for personal expenses. They each decided what they wanted to buy or had someone designated to do such shopping for them. For the sisters, that someone was Tom and I. We kept track of the money coming in each month, and what was spent on them.

"Is Santa Clause here yet?" Marie couldn't seem to calm down, and it was Christmas Eve.

"No, because you are still awake and out of bed." I could hear Ruth trying to get her to go to bed.

"That's right, we have to be asleep when he comes." Marie had worked this process the way we wanted her to. She got herself ready for bed.

"I come to say good night to you," Janet stood at the counter, offering out her hands for me to touch.

"Okay, thank you. Go on to bed", I knew this wouldn't work. "I wanna love you." She leaned against the counter until her hands were touching my nose as I sat charting.

I stood up and leaned over the counter, giving her a hug. As always, I had to pry her arms off my shoulders.

"That's good Janet, now go on to bed, please." I pointed down the hall toward her room and sat down again.

"I want to kiss your hands", she was unflappable in her mission.

"This is your last goodnight." I tried to sound firm as I put out my hands so she could kiss the back of both of them.

"Okay, good night", and she headed down the hall.

Christmas Day was very busy. Everybody was energized to get everyone up and to the dining room for breakfast. After breakfast, all the presents would be handed out. We even had a Santa Clause to come in and give out the presents. The residents were at various levels of excitement, but Marie and Janet were wired.

"Look what I got", Marie showed me a stuffed bear. I remembered picking it off the shelf at Good Will.

"Wow, what a great bear!" I responded.

"Janet got a doggie and I got a bear", Marie was quick to compare. Janet came up with her stuffed doggie, and I gave as many ooos and aaahs as I could. I was taking video photos of the present opening, hoping to get left out of the one on-one-stuff. The staff was great helping open boxes and gush over every single present.

At one point I was watching the sisters, sitting side by side at their dining table. They each had a present in their hands, turning it over and over, gazing at it as if enthralled. Quietly showing their treasure to each other while the rest of the room finished opening presents and slowly moving out of the dining room to their individual rooms.

"Know what I got from Santa Claus?" Janet caught me in the office while I was completing physician orders. She didn't wait for my reply.

"I got a doggie, and a red shirt and a blue shirt. And some underpants and two bras. The bras are white. But the underpants are, uh, pink, and blue, white and one has flowers on it. Wanna see them?

"I already saw them when you opened them", I said. "Huhn?"

"I saw what Santa Clause gave you, remember?", I was now "Come on, I'll show ye" she took my hand and walked me to her room where she laid everything on the bed. "See, isn't that nice?"

"Yes it is, and you need to find safe places for everything, so they stay nice." I nodded about everything and quietly slipped out to the hall while she began to put her new things away.

Christmas is also a day when the kitchen goes all out to serve the traditional turkey meal. Tom helps in the kitchen, and I help serve. The dining room is a buzz of activity while we serve every resident as much as they wanted of what they wanted. Only Robert wanted a peanut butter and jelly sandwich instead.

Lunch was served starting at 11:57am, and everyone was stuffed, heading back to their rooms by 12:45pm. Staff worked at cleaning up the dining room. By 1: 15pm the building was quiet, like it gets at 1:15Am.

"Everyone is in bed, and sound asleep"; Ruth smiled as she dropped dirty clothing down the laundry chute

"Yep, all the tryptophan in the turkey helped them all get sleepy. "Well, I think I'll take my break now, because this quiet cannot last more than about 20 minutes.

I remember walking down the hall about 2:30pm, and most of our residents were still in their beds, sleeping. And why not, it was a big day for everyone.

The building smelled of turkey, dressing, rolls and cranberry sauce. Its buzz of activity with the presents was replaced with quiet snoring in each hall. I thought it was a great way to end a great day.

"Moron, functional imbecile," is how their oldest history and physical evaluations are read. Words no one would even think of using today as part of a medical or psychological assessment. But in 1938, when they were given to the State of Oregon, those were educated words documented by professionals who evaluated Janet and Marie when they were each around 7 years old.

I read that evaluation several times and began to see a hazy family setting. Born in Lyons, Oregon; neither Janet nor Marie was able to complete second grade. There is a vague reference to the mother not having much intelligence. There may have even been a third girl that was given up and later taken back.

Both girls went to the state mental health hospital in the late thirties. When a dedicated institution was built in the 1940s, meant for long term care to profoundly mentally impaired people, they may have been two of the first new residents.

The histories speak of angry outbursts, learning to do basic tasks such as making their beds, cleaning up their table settings, and dressing, that sort of thing. At times they lived together and other times they were in different cabins.

In the late 70s they were each sent to smaller group homes, with little information from that care.

Then in 1982 and 1985 they each came to Ellendale Home. At no time did anyone connected to their family come looking for them. Evidently, when they were moved out to smaller group homes, someone tried to figure out where the parents were. The only entry was "it appears the mother moved to Texas, where exactly is not available."

On all our records, Marie is Janet's next of kin and Janet is Marie's next of kin. Over the years, the State of Oregon has actually become their parents. So, who makes decisions for them? An imaginary panel of the primary physician, Senior Services Case Manager, care home Administrator, Mental Health physician and whomever else is also involved with their care at the moment. And because the sisters can't really understand any part of long-term planning, that professional group agonizes over the questions.

We had to update Advanced Directives of both of them. I suggested we ask for a guardian, but there is no reason for the legal system to appoint someone to make the decisions. Mainly because there is no pay. Before we finalized the paperwork, I called the case manager and the physician. We agreed to agree with No Life Sustaining Measures. But we could have the sisters sign their forms or make a statement that they were advised of the decision and understood the decision. With most issues, they can't understand.

Because RCF levels of care in Oregon do not require a RN as part of the staff, I am not prepared to give up my other private contract work to devote full time nursing care. In fact, I really didn't want to spend much time in the facility at all. My husband was very excited to learn the ropes as an Administrator. However, after working with long-term care facilities for years as a nurse, I wanted to stay as detached as possible to the daily care needs of the residents. I wanted to support Tom's enthusiasm at having our own business and his learning a new field. His charisma and gregarious manner are genuine because he enjoys people, people, people.

I, on the other hand, am an introvert's introvert. I don't 'dislike' people. I'm just as content doing my work without a lot of personal interaction. I knew from my time with Hospice how close someone under my care might get. I didn't want to deal with that again, not with 40 people under my care. My plan was to be the 'detail nursing resource' and let Tom develop his team as he wanted. Then I can be free to do my own contract work and keep myself detached.

Detached my ass. It was a great theory, and I should have known better. What one resists one becomes. But I was not going easily into that warm world of caring for those with mental health AND aging needs.

My visits are short and to the point. When I plan to work on chart entries or reviews the chart room door is closed, no time for interactions from residents. I want them to work with the staff well and see me only as The Nurse. That way, staff will learn to interact on their own and develop their own styles of working with our residents. I shut the office door often to have quiet. And almost as if she knew my plan to keep her at bay, that office door opened often.

"Will you braid my hair?" she asks, holding out a hairbrush with one hand and three hair clips with the other.

"Ask Karen, Janet. I'm doing something I can't stop right now", I didn't want to get in the habit of doing direct care at any time.

"Hunh?" she asked

I notice she leans forward at about a 25-degree angle. From the back, I can see her feet moving in heavy fashionable tennis shoes, slightly pigeon toed. Her legs are very thin, and her pants have little contour because she has very little butt.

I'm trying to go about my business for the day, trying to get as much done as possible and leave. I am driven to keep the staff from relying on me to make decisions. I'm not available on site on a regular schedule. So, the staff need to solve problems for themselves, relying only on calling me if no options fix whatever problem they face.

We turned one of the resident rooms into the chart room and a mini office. The computer is there, with the idea that since this office was on the back hall, staff charting there would be able to monitor what was happening at that part of the building. This also means that when I am there to do charting, etc., I'm in that office alone. Again, reality meets concept.

I am at the computer, trying to complete assessments. But Janet sees me there and comes to talk to me.

"High, you look nice today", one of her standard greetings.

"Thank you, Janet, now go find something to do, please, I'm trying to get work done here," I'm trying to be kind yet firm.

"No, I'm working"

"Hunh?"

"Not now, please go find something to do." I stood up, escorted her out of the office, came back in and shut the door.

Getting down to documenting the assessment on a new resident, I'm just about done when the office door opens.

"See the bear my sister gives me? It's white and the ribbon is green. Do you like it?"

Janet is holding a stuffed bear and pointing to all the different colors she finds on it."

"Yes, it's a nice bear, very white. But I need to work, so I need you to go somewhere else for now", I am trying not to hurt her feelings.

"See the ribbon, it has two colors. This part is blue and this part is green."

"Yes, I see that, very nice"

"Which color is your favorite?" she holds the bear out to me.

"I like green, that's my favorite", I move the bear back to her.

"Hunh?" Janet asks

"Green", I shout, getting closer to her ear to speak.

From out in the hall Nancy came in, took Janet by the arm and escorted her away to the dining room to color. I turned back to the computer and the charting I needed to get done.

The door opened and Marie came in. She stood by the side of the desk, looking toward the ceiling behind me. She has a habit of cocking her head to the right, with her chin down and her eyes looking up. This is her 'notice me' stance.

She'd changed her shirt, and I was to notice it and compliment her again.

"Marie, I need you not to come into a room if the door is closed." I was not going to let either one of them get away with barging in wherever they wanted. It seemed essential to me that they learn more appropriate manners as of NOW.

"Do you like my blouse?" Marie asked with her husky voice.

"Yes, it's a nice blouse, very pretty. Now go on, I have work to do."

She turned and walked out of the office and again I made sure the door was closed behind her.

I finished the charting I needed to do but began to feel trapped in that office. I couldn't open the door, because on the other side would be Janet or Marie or both, waiting for my attention. I was not going to let them interrupt my work. Which is why I had answered questions and closed the office door six times in 20 minutes. My 'focused work style' was certainly working!

"Marie just nailed Sara in the dining room. She's been angry all morning and after breakfast walked over and hit Sara on the shoulder." The charge aide called me with this information.

"Any idea what caused the outburst?" I ask, detached by the phone line.

"Yes, well no. She got upset with Sara at breakfast because Sara got two eggs and she only had one. It's been downhill since then."

"Does she have medication ordered for agitation?" I asked. "Yes, and I gave her one at breakfast. I knew this was coming."

The Charge Aide was Andrew, who worked so well with the residents.

"Well, I guess the only other thing to do is watch her and not let her get near Sara again today." I had no other words of wisdom.

"Okay, we'll work on that."

Neither sister was within my vision as I walked down to the chart room. I was lucky to have an hour or two before my next appointment. I wanted to update chart notes, and was halfway through the oldest ones when I could hear ...

"Sam's a bastard, I hate him", the unmistakable husky monotone of Marie. As I listened, I could hear her footsteps around the corner and move toward her room. "I hate him, he's a shit."

Getting up, I decided to try and defuse whatever was upsetting her.

"Marie, I'm hearing very rude words from you. What is the problem?"

She stood in the doorway to her room, arms at her side, her mouth tight so her chin jutted out. Her eyes looked far right, and she didn't answer me.

"Why are you angry at Sam?" I tried not to sound like a parent.

"He didn't let me win Bingo. I hate him", her voice was a husky whisper.

"Remember when we talked about playing games?" I tried to keep my voice soft. "If you play games, sometimes you might not win. If you are going to get upset when you don't win, then you can't play."

"I don't care; Sam's a bastard"

"Did you hit Sara?" She nodded, saying nothing

"Why, what did Sara do that upset you?" Again, I'm trying to sound calm and soft.

"She got two eggs at breakfast, and I only got one." The change of victims also brought a change in voice tone. Marie's voice was higher and clear.

"Did you hit Sara because of the eggs?" I am very direct now.

"She got two eggs." Marie obviously believed the action was justified.

"That was a very bad thing to do, Marie. The kitchen decides how many eggs to give out, not Sara. And hurting someone for any reason is not good. You need to go down and apologize to Sara."

"No, she got two eggs," the chin began to put forward again. "Then you need to go to your room until you are ready to apologize to Sara." I pointed toward her bed and motioned her to go into her room.

"No, I'm not going to. I don't want to." Her eyes turned to the floor. Her shoulders drooped.

Without putting a hand on her, I continued to point to her room. She started to take a step to the side, and I met her step. After a few seconds of deep breathing, she turned and went to her bed. I shut the door.

I was back at the computer when the sound of a slamming door caught up with me. Marie likes to slam doors.

I finished the rest of my charting, about 15 minutes later. After shutting down the computer, I knocked on Marie's door and opened it slightly. She was sleeping, curled up on her bed. I gently closed the door and went to other tasks.

Lunchtime was nearing, and Nancy went down to remind residents of the time. I heard her talking to Marie as they came down the hall. I took that as my cue to complete the consequence part of Marie's kicking Sara.

"Marie, are you feeling better now?" I asked her

"Yes", her voice was again that husky whisper.

"Before you sit down for lunch, you need to go and apologize to Sara for hitting her." I knew my voice sounded very firm, and I meant it to.

"I don't want to", she said, looking at the floor.

"Sara didn't want to be hit. So now you go and apologize." I pointed to Sara sitting on her bed waiting for lunch. "Come on, I'll go with you."

"I'm sorry", the voice was barely audible now.

"Nope, not to me, to Sara", I'm a rock of consequence now. We stepped into Sara's room. She looked at me and then Marie with her usual expressionless face. She began to stare at Marie, watching every move.

"I'm sorry I hit you", Marie said softly.

"Sara, did you hear Marie? She is apologizing to you for hitting you this morning. Is that okay", I knew I would get no verbal answer.

"Marie, you can go to lunch now. But remember, no more hurting anyone, ever again." Marie walked proudly to her place in the dining room.

Janet and Marie each and together taught us their rules of social graces. It is based on numbers and desire. After several months of trying to understand why they seem to 'target' other residents, Tom finally figured it out.

Breakfast can set up the day for anyone anywhere. At Ellendale Home, a good day starts with everyone enjoying breakfast and leaving the table calm. To better ensure this outcome, we've learned the basics of Janet/Marie processing. They both like two eggs. With Janet, newly diagnosed with diabetes, she has only one egg. However, she will look at the other plates being served and count eggs. If Sara or Clara at the table next to her has 2 eggs, we are not going to have a good day.

At a staff meeting, we talked through this issue, because the staff is as frustrated with having to run interference because of 'eggs'. The kitchen staff was stumped by the problem, although they did not have to deal with the hitting and name-calling directly.

"They don't know about sizes, but they know numbers." Karen offered her observations.

"They always look at Sara and Clara's plates and compare", came from John.

"How about cutting Sara and Clara's eggs before taking out to the table? That way they can't count anything?" Marie sounded logical in her approach. The kitchen crew was willing.

"Okay, now how about pancakes? Do the same thing?" I ventured.

"Sure," Becky made the idea seem obvious.

"Any other food items we need to solve problems with the sisters?" Tom's words hung over the group as everyone seemed to mentally walks through daily meal options, searching for potential problems.

"Yes, hot dogs." I can't remember who said it; we all knew it was an ever-looming threat.

Tom and I work out the menus weekly, and although we do not serve hot dogs weekly, they pop onto the menu about twice a month. With Janet's new diabetes, this simple food becomes so complicated for everyone else. The sister's love their hot dogs.

"Janet is only supposed to have one hot dog and technically only half a bun." Jean seemed to cook most often when hot dogs were the faire.

"And she always wants a second dog", Andrew added.

"Marie also wants two every time. So, if we give her seconds, Janet will be ballistic. And if we don't let Marie have seconds, she will be in a foul mood the rest of the day." Karen spoke from experience.

"Okay, so how do we solve this one? I don't think we have to be so exact with one meal. Can we serve one each and then when they want seconds tell them only one is left, they can share?" I hoped someone else had a better option.

"Sure, the kitchen can do that. You just must be sure no one else gets seconds after them. They'll know we lied." Karen warned.

The meeting ended with everyone feeling armed for battle in the dining room. Tom and I made sure Hot Dogs were on next week's menu so we could try out all the suggestions.

"Can I have another hot dog?" Marie was at the kitchen doorway.

"No, darlin, we only have one left. Does Janet want seconds?"

"Yes, she does." Marie said as Janet walked up with her plate

"Do you want to share the last one?" Becky was trying to make this work.

"Okay" from Marie

The Hot Dog was cut in half and placed on each plate.

"Need a bun" Marie held up her plate.

"No more buns, we ran out. "Becky said

"Over there are buns", Marie pointed to a plate with three buns next to the stove.

"Those aren't good, too old to eat," Becky hustled them back to their table.

"I thought I was cooking when Marie saw those damn buns on the plate." Becky sounded exhausted as she sat down for her break.

"Well, just remember, they are retarded but they aren't stupid. We just have to stay one step ahead."

I was standing with my back toward the long hall of the facility. Sharon handed me the phone, and as I talked to a hospital nurse, I could feel fingers jabbing me in the ribs. I turned to see Marie holding her hands out toward me, smiling and hoping for my smile.

"I tickled you", she said with a giggle

"Yes, don't do that while I'm on the phone" I held my hand up with one extended finger and wagged it back and forth. I turned back to the counter and resumed my phone conversation.

"Ouch," I said abruptly. The tickling fingers had turned into pinchers. Marie had pinched me in the ribs, and it hurt! I turned around and glared at her.

"You a funny woman, Marie laughed at me.

"Marie, stop pinching, that hurts." I was firm and indignant. I was on an important phone call.

"Can we do hearts?" Marie's husky voice passed my ear.

"Yes, you can do hearts." I replied and watched Millie's face droop.

"Go get your crayons, and I'll bring down some hearts for you to color." I asked her "Go to your office?" Janet asked, with a smile across her toothless mouth. "Can we color in your office?"

"Yes, I'll meet you there in a few minutes. They headed off to their rooms to get their colors.

"I'm tired of hearts, they're everywhere", Millie emoted by putting her hands to her temples.

"Well, take a chill pill, because we have 3 weeks before Valentine's Day, and the sisters will probably want to color hearts every day. And I won't get much done because they will be in the chart room all that time."

'Fell and hit her face on the edge of the sink.' I read the incident report from the night before. Janet got up to go to the bathroom, walked 15 feet to the room next door. Evidently, she got dizzy when getting up from the commode. Trying to catch herself, she got off balance and fell.

Looking at her face, I could tell she had hit the sink, hard.

Her left eye was swollen, darkest at the crest of the eye socket.

Within 24 hours she could hardly see out of that eye, and the purple was moving down her cheek.

We were all feeling awful about the bruise. We seemed to warn any and everyone who came to visit, hoping to decrease the shock of Janet's face.

Over the month, her eye changed like a very slow chameleon.

All month, the eye became frightening as it changed from black/purple to purple/green and then to green/yellow.

She's been stumbling and falling frequently for over a year.

At first, we thought it was the shoes she wore. She'd gotten heavy tennis shoes from somewhere, and they were very awkward for her to walk in. We changed them to deck shoes that she didn't have to pick up so high when walking. But the problem of falls is very present anyway.

One day the Mental Health Case Managers came in for a visit, and I let them know about Janet's eye. Carol looked aghast when Janet came in to say hello.

"Oh my, doesn't she need to see a doctor?"

"What would the doctor do?" her companion Ellen asked.

"Well, I guess I don't know. Do we have to do a protective service investigation on this?"

"Protective Service? It is my responsibility to report such issues. We know how she felt, we address this in the care plans, and the doctor knows. What would be investigated?" I tried to sound informative and not irritated.

"Carol, this fall is a result of medical issues, not mental health. I think they've take care of it fine. Janet seems to be healing." Ellen helped with her comments.

Carol was a new case manager, having transferred from the large institutional home for developmentally disabled. Admittedly, she was used to a very rigid system. As the case manager, she was involved with broader care issues now and working with clients in many different living situations.

Janet walks leaning forward, bent at the hip. She does not see well. I suggested at one time we have her eyes checked for glasses.

"She has glasses already", Penny told me.

"Where are they?" I was surprised by this information

"Ask her, she keeps them very safe"

"Janet, where are your glasses?", I turned to face her.

"Want to see 'me? I'll go get them and show you." She showed me they were tucked in her dresser drawer under her pink pajamas, in their case. She put them on so I could see them. And just as carefully, she put them in the case and back in the dresser. I asked her why she did not wear them. She was clear, she did not want them to get 'broke or anything.' Try as I could, I could not seem to explain to her why the glasses could help.

"Is my sister going to be alright?", Marie asked daily.

Marie was also falling, getting dizzy and unsteady on her feet. This was a newer problem for her, and we could not figure out what was causing the problem.

Since Janet was newly diagnosed with diabetes, we assumed Marie would have the same problem. We thought perhaps she'd started showing diabetic signals; however, we could not do regular testing with her. Dr. Munson has given us an order to check Marie's blood sugar in the morning and evening for 5 days. We were certain we would see a genetic connection to her older sister. Marie would have none of it.

Every 3 months, three of us would work with Marie, and hold her arm so enough blood could be drawn to do lab tests because of the anti-seizure medications she was taking. The rest of the day we all endured her angry slamming of doors, stomping and yelling. So, we were pretty sure having her finger stuck 2x/day was also not going to be acceptable.

The first morning, Marie raised a fuss right away. She held her hands in fists and jammed them into her pockets. Her voice, difficult to understand at best, boomed a monotone response of "No" heard by many within the hallway she stood in. Twice a day we negotiated with her, and a few times she was coaxed into letting us check her blood sugar. However, we did not have a clear picture of why she was falling from the infrequent tests.

We'd set Marie up for a CT Scan and MRI in the past 2 months. We tried to explain to the neurologist that Marie would need something to calm her down for an MRI. Valium 5mg was ordered to be taken ½ hour before the scan. I called the neurologist's office and spoke with the RN, stating that Marie would need more than one 5mg dose of Valium.

"Dr. Palla, I know that this little bit of Valium will not enough for you to complete the test." I was hopeful this physician would listen.

"Oh, the staff in the CT Scan room are very good with people showing apprehension," came the soft, gentle brush off I expected.

"Dr. Palla, please understand that I want this test to work for Marie. And I also know this resident." I found it frustrating that the MD was blowing off my experience with her patient.

"Oh, I see that she is mentally retarded. I will let the imagine staff know so they can speak with her simply."

"She cannot understand anything of why this test is done. For instance, last fall we had an order for a mammogram to be done. Because she did not understand anything about the machines or the clamping device; when her breast was smashed to a certain point that it hurt her, she pulled herself out of the device." I was trying to get a point across.

"Oh, my. Well, maybe we should increase that Valium to 10 mg. Will there be someone coming with her for this test?" Dr. Palla sounded as if my words meant something, however small.

"Yes, we will have a staff member with her. But that person may have to be with her, physically touching her during the entire test."

We sent Millie, who had a good rapport with Marie. Millie had to lie next to her on a gurney for an ultrasound and then keep her hand on Marie's leg during the MRI. The Valium wore off before the testing was done. We tried to tell people, but what do we know.

They were back in time for lunch, but Millie looked like she needed a liquid lunch. Marie was very excited.

'They took a really big picture." She let everyone know. And she got a sucker after the picture.

We truly hoped that scan would show something we could work around. No luck. Within 2 weeks we got a report. The tests showed nothing abnormal. That was the good news. However, we still did not know what the problem was that was the bad news.

I become very irritated with the repeated questions, over and over the same phrase. Sometimes I'm reminded of the movie "Ground Hog Day' because every morning when you walk into work, they meet you with the same litany.

"Hi, how are you? You look very nice today."

Easter was coming, and that meant new color schemes and more things to do outside the building. We set up plastic eggs with dyed real eggs.

"Time to plan for the Easter Bunny." I was again talking to everyone in a staff meeting.

"I think we should dye eggs and hide em. All that stuff." Jenny announced.

"Who would actually do the boiling of eggs and coloring without a huge mess?" asked Tom.

"The kitchen can boil the eggs. And we can set up the dye for the eggs. We can do the dying as an activity out on the deck." Jenny seemed to have this all settled in her head.

"One of the problems we had last year was all the candy laying about. With four diabetics, we need a better plan."

"Okay, let's also use plastic eggs." That sounded good. "How does that solve the candy issue?" I asked.

There was a lull in the brainstorming, because Easter equals candy.

"I know, let's have them bring their plastic eggs up to be traded in for candy. Then we can have diabetic candy for the diabetics." John seemed to have a logical response once again.

"Okay, we need to have the eggs ready by Thursday, so they will be ready to hide on Saturday. Night shift gets to hide them." Tom outlined.

"I think we need a real Easter Bunny". Millie suggested.

"Who gets stuck with that one", John asked her

"I'll do it, I'll get a suit rented and be here Easter morning right after breakfast is over."

The plan worked great. Millie was there in costume as the Easter Bunny. Tom took photos of everyone. The morning was a huge success. As we all go ready for lunch at noon, the nephew of one of our residents came in for a short visit and left a sack of unknown treasures with her. Staff were getting residents down for the meal, the kitchen was starting to serve, and I was rolling out the medication cart to give everyone their noon medications.

I'd given medication to one of the residents sitting near the middle of the dining room and had my back toward the east entrance. I'd bent over to help Richr3rd open his Ensure when something pink sped past my head and landed on the floor. I straightened up to see what nearly hit me when another pink missile struck the back of Richard's chair.

"In coming", frank shouted.

I turned just in time to see Georgia hurl another candy egg across the room. Karen was trying to get through the chairs to her and stop the barrage before someone lost an eye. I tried to calm Richard, who mentioned something about howitzers, while Karen explained to Georgia the problem with throwing the candy. She offered to give out the candy that was left.

The rest of the meal was smooth, and I was back in the medication station putting things away when I heard commotion again. Janet was yelling and chasing after Karen.

"She got one of the chocolates by mistake, and when I took it away from her, she exploded," Karen's face showed this wasn't a game.

"She's got my candy", Janet announced.

"You can't have candy, you have diabetes", Karen tried to explain.

I decided to let this one work through without me and returned to my medication cart.

"I want candy", a loud, upset Janet kept yelling from the doorway of the dining room.

I went into the hall, prepared to deal with a 'bad girl' problem. What I saw was 145 pounds of elderly woman, leaning against the wall crying ... no ... sobbing because she wanted some candy. I walked up to her. "You can't have candy now because it will make you sick." I said.

"I want some candy. She took my candy." The tears continued

"Candy will make you sick" I tried giving her a hug.

"Everybody else got some, I want some," the words were garbled by the sobs, but she was clear enough.

"Come on, I'll walk you to your room so you can rest", I put one arm around her shoulders while walking down the hall. At her room, I helped her sit on the bed, and I again reminded her that she can't eat candy."

"I want some candy. Marie got candy. I was good, I want candy." Her voice was somewhat calmer, but she was obviously not going to give up.

"There is no way she can understand why she can't have candy," I thought to myself as I walked back down the hall. I saw Karen wiping the dining room tables.

"Any of that candy left? I asked

"Yes, I put it on the counter there", she pointed while continuing to spray and wipe. "Did you win against Janet? Is she calmed down?"

"No, I don't think I can change her mind without chocolate."

I began to unwrap one of the singe pieces of milk chocolate, while Karen came to my side. I broke the chocolate in half, put one half in my mouth and rewrapped the other half in the foil.

"You going to give her that?" Karen asked

"Yep, there is no way I want to spend all day with her broken-hearted tantrums over a small piece of candy. So, we'll see how good my negotiations are." I left the dining room for Janet's room as Karen agreed with my techniques.

"Whatever makes life easier for all of us, go for it." She chuckled.

I slowly opened the door of Janet's bedroom. She was still sitting on the side of her bed. She wasn't crying any more, but was looking at her hands, wiggling her fingers. She looked up as the door continued to open and looked at me. Immediately she noticed I had something in my hand.

"Is that my candy?" She asked

"Yes, you can have one piece, like everyone else." I held out the foil wrapper to her. She took the candy, looked at it for a few seconds, and then opened it. "Thank you", she sang to me.

I slipped out again while she was unwrapping the foil.

It might not be on the same level as Near East Negotiations, I thought; but for the world inside this facility, keeping the piece with one bit of chocolate is a true blessing.

I feel very inept being an effective nurse at times. I can understand, even experience the process of aging, making changes by choice or happenstance year after year. I've got plenty of experience working with someone angry, in despair, frustration or calm acceptance of physical limitations and losses. Crossing my 50th birthday, you might say, "I have met the patient, and they are me".

Not one page my nursing texts give me much wisdom in planning nursing care for Septuagenarian women with pre-schoolers minds.

If I let myself dwell on this for too long, I'll scare myself away. But how do I help Janet understand why simple changes in her life must happen now that she has diabetes?

Janet will only let us use one finger, the same finger for her blood sugar testing. I'm afraid we're going to wear it out.

"Let me use that other finger", I try to coax her

"No, this one," Janet pointed at her left ring finger.

"Isn't that one hurting from being poked?"

"This one", she was charming with her direction I gave in.

I walked down the hall, around the corner and knocked on Marie's door. I was looking for her sister, Janet; who was a newly diagnosed diabetic. It was time to check her blood sugar before dinner. I found her helping Marie make her bed.

"I want to go for a walk to the park," Janet was clear in her request.

"We weren't going to the park today, Janet," Millie responded

"I want to go to the park," Janet repeated, leaning toward Millie as if that would make it happen.

"What's in the park?", Millie asked

"A swing, I want to swing," Janet's face lit up.

"Maybe after lunch, we might go after lunch".

"Hunh?"

"Maybe after lunch," Millie echoed to her

"Okay", Janet smiled up at me like a caricature of Puck and headed down the hall.

Today was probably going to be a very awful day. Just like any battalion getting ready to take the hill", we were planning to clean Marie's room. I don't mean making the bed, sweep the floor, and picking up glasses type of clean. I mean, retrieve months of treasures she'd accumulated.

Well, it was sort of her fault. She'd shown Karen her dresser drawer that was broken. The front of the drawer had pulled out where the small nails went into the sidepieces. Karen could see the main reason was the drawer being crammed with 'stuff'. She told Marie to take all her things out of that drawer so it could be fixed. While Marie carefully emptied her drawer, Karen came to me with the suggestion that we now try and get some of the clutter out of Marie's room.

Suddenly we heard Marie's husky voice with an added squeak at the end. "Help Me, Help me". We found Marie on the floor at the end of her bed. Her walker was wrapped around her, and she was laying on the floor.

"I fell", she said.

"As we picked her up and untangled her from the walker, I could hear this 'Mother Voice' coming from my mouth.

"Why did you bring the walker into your room? It makes you fall." I picked up the walker and put it out in the hall next to her door.

"I'm sorry." Marie looked at the floor

"I'm sorry too. I don't want you to keep falling. Why don't you go lay down in the other room while we get this cleaned up?"

"She won't stay away long" Karen observed. "I could take her down for her shower now."

This was the point of planning the assault on the hill.

"Okay, you take her to the shower. Becky and I will clean the room,"

I was confident we'd have enough time.

As Marie headed to the shower at the other end of the building, Becky and I began to pull out all the drawers in her dresser. We found old (I mean concrete) candy bars, plastic sacks, and something powdery in a box that smelled somewhat like potato chips. The bottom drawer would not push in all the way. I found underwear, bras, books and stuffed toys that had fallen behind it.

We found magazines stacked orderly in a tower next to the dresser. I pulled all of them out, finding children's books among the magazines. But after that tower of magazines was gone, I found another one inside the closet. She also had some 60 stuffed animals in bags in her closet. Some she hadn't looked at in months. But we couldn't navigate the closet well because of the clothing.

The closet is about six feet wide and 2 feet deep. The hanging pole was bending with the weight.

"What are you doing in my closet", the raspy voice broke my amazed thought processes.

We'd been busted cleaning her room. I turned and saw Marie's face, snuggled in her fluffy blue robe.

"Oh, don't you look squeaky clean now?" I changed the subject.

"Did you use lotion?"

"Yes" she held up her hands for me to sniff.

Karen stepped in and diverted her to another room to get dressed. We then talked again about what to do with all the stuff in Marie's room. She could not understand that all the clutter would be a fire hazard. Or that having small items on the floor of her room made hazards for her falling. We'd removed 6 apple box loads of magazines and books. We'd filled three large trash bags with trash from her drawers. And 7 bags of stuffed toys from the back of the closet.

The next part of the plan was the clothing issue. While Julie kept Marie busy in another room, Karen went into the closet and took out about a third of the clothing, items she'd never seen Marie wear. They were taken across the hall to the office, where we could fold them behind closed doors.

"You brat, your snot", Marie yelled at me as I passed her room.

"You're a son of a bitch".

I just kept on walking. Today, I was all those things.

"Trisha, this is Brenda. Tom wanted me to call and let you know, Marie fell again. That's three times today." Brenda's tone of voice sounded frustrated and worried.

"Call the MD and tell him we either need her seen in his office, or we send her to ER to be checked up." I sighed as I held up the phone.

Tom was very concerned, I knew. Marie already had a bruise on her right temple from an earlier fall. They were all in her room now. We'd changed her shoes. She was using the walker, but not effectively. She could not understand why someone needed to be with her when she did something. AND, there was the possibility she was developing diabetes like Janet.

Tom worried about liability if they got badly hurt. I was not. But we had to be sure everything was documented. I knew our serviced plans, which had been signed by the case manager, addressed the issue that both women were falling, and unable to understand or follow directions to be more safe. We'd discussed the options. They did not need licensed nursing help. A nursing home would not be able to keep them from falling unless they were tied in a chair. That was not going to be done anywhere anyway. They'd lived in this one building since 1982, for almost 20 years. We know if we moved one, we would have to move both.

"Did Marie get back from the ER?" I asked John.

"Yes, they didn't send much, just a few orders. No new medications."

"Okay, I'll look at them tomorrow." I wasn't surprised. When I got to the home, I found the papers from the ER. Get a UA (urinalysis sample), continue to use walker, call for PT/OT evaluation. That was all.

"Marie, wait, Marie" I could hear Becky's voice get louder just before the crash. Heading out of the office, down the hall, I found Marie again on the floor, walker surrounding her, partly entangled in a wheel chair. The loudest part of the crash was the wheelchair hitting the wall as it tipped over.

Again, she was not hurt. Three of us worked on the tangle of equipment and body apart. We all hugged Marie, and I walked her to her room to lie down.

"She ran the walker straight into the wheelchair." Becky told me. "It was like she couldn't see it. And when she bumped into it, instead of moving the walker away from the wheelchair she just kept pushing until the whole thing fell over."

"Millie, can we get Marie in for an eye check up?" I asked, hoping there was another option for Marie's independence and safety.

"She goes on Wednesday, already have the appointment", Millie, ever efficient, ever wonderful.

Thursday morning, I walked into Ellendale, checking in with the crew. Millie, coming from down the hallway, needed to talk with me.

"Marie is blind in one eye, and can only see about 20/50 in the other one. The doctor told me her new glasses would help some, but she may lose vision in the other eye in another year."

"When does she get the new glasses"? I asked "They'll call when ready, probably Friday." Millie's expression looked as concerned as I felt.

"We need to connect with the blind commission or someone who can help us plan for her blindness. And we need to have Janet's eyes checked too.

That explained many of the falls, not seeing hazards on the floor of her room, not having good special concepts, not seeing other large items in the hallways. Even more, it seemed moving her would be a bad idea. She knows where everything is at Ellendale Home.

Two days later Marie had her new glasses. She wouldn't wear the old one, but these seemed to be much better. She told us she could see more. And she posed with them on for everyone to see and admire her.

Then she fell again. But she didn't push her walker into another piece of equipment, and she didn't have her walker in her room, she was trying to get something out of her closet, slipped on the edge of her bedspread and bumped into the closet door jamb. We know the glasses will only 'help' her see well.

"We need to call someone in from the Blind Commission," I suggested to Millie over the phone. See if someone will come out and help us solve this problem.

The representative from the Commission for the Blind was wonderful. She'd worked with severely mentally retarded before going to the Commission.

It really is important that Marie stays here as her sight fades. She knows the layout of the building, recognizes other residents and staff. It is very important staff learn to work with her to maintain safety.

She suggested some changes in lighting, re-painting the handrails along the walls so they are more contrasting against the walls.

May 23rd, Marie's birthday. We will have cake and soda at 3pm. Every month we celebrate the birthdays for that month with one birthday party. In May, this year, Marie's is the last birthday of the month.

"I got a party today", she was telling me. Cause my birthday is today. How old am I?" She had her hands together in front of her chest.

"Today you are 73 years old", I told her.

"Wow, 73. That's big", she grinned and repeated it twice. Then she went into the dining room to tell the residents sitting in front of the TV.

"Can I ask you something" Janet stood next to me as I placed dirty dishes in the cart after lunch.

"Yes, ask me" I replied, not looking toward her.

"I bumped into my arm, and it hurts. I didn't pick at it or anything. It hurts. I bumped it into the wall. It hurts. I need band aid."

I looked at the arm she was offering me as evidence. There was a slightly reddened area, nothing else.

"No band aid, your skin is too fragile. And with your diabetes, we need to not use tape on it unless we really need to." I knew I was blowing smoke.

"I didn't pick it or anything. But it hurts and I need a band-aid on it. See, I didn't do nothin'," she was negotiating with heart.

"No band aide" I said, firmly and loudly because of her hearing. "Let the air heal it and leave it alone."

Her face frowned, and she walked away from me still holding her elbow up. I finished cleaning up the last tables in the dining room and could hear Janet talking to the Millie at the desk. Same litany, same request for a band-aide. Millie didn't give in either. No band aide.

After several tries, Janet seemed to give up the idea of a band aide.

The phone rang, Millie answered it, and I went to the kitchen. "Janet, give that back. You know better than to come into the medication station." Millie sounded surprised. I went to the med station just in time to see Janet being walked out of the med area by Karen.'

"You don't love me anymore. You don't care", Janet was unhappy.

"What was that about?" I asked warily.

"She came back here and got a band aide out of the jar. I was on the phone with the lab, and she just walked in, went right to the jar and got the band aide." Millie tried to hide the laugh that was trying to get out.

"Lordy, I guess she really wanted a band-aide." I had no wisdom for this one. But I took the jar with the band aides and put it in the locked cupboard under the counter. Millie was already writing about the incident in the communications log.

The 4th of July was coming, and there were lots of flags around the building. We have 6 veterans living at Ellendale Home. It is very important to them that we show acknowledgement of the 4th.

"Are we going to have fireworks?", one of the staff asked.

"No, not even sparklers. We tried that last year and about set both sisters afire." I did not want to think about the process again. "What happened?"

"We were still new at this, and Tom thought it would be great for sparklers in the front courtyard. He had water in a bucket and was surrounded by six residents wanting to sparkle. For just an instance his attention was drawn away from the sisters, who stood holding their sparklers. Then Marie dropped hers, and when Janet bent down to pick it up, she touched Marie's skirt hem with her sparkler. Well, you can imagine, the skirt fizzed, Marie said, "Help, I'm on fire". Janet straightened up to see, and dropped her hand to her side, putting a hole in her shirt.

"Was anyone hurt?"

"Only Tom. He grabbed the sparkler at the wrong end to get it away from Janet. The girls thought it was great and finished the night watching everyone else make patterns with their sparklers.

"Whoa, that sounds like a near dis-ass-ter".

"Thank you. And don't ask Tom about it. He's kind of touchy on the subject."

Paperwork will always be the bane of nursing. As the resource for nursing issues, I am determined to do LESS paperwork, not more. We must re-evaluate the individual needs of each resident every 6 months. That evaluation needs to be very detailed. The theory is that someone who has never been in the facility or seen the residents can get a clear picture of the residents and their care needs. Reality is that a dozen people can give care day in, and day out and STILL not have a clear picture of their needs.

I was trying to get some paperwork done, evaluations for the next service plan meeting. Janet wanted to color, and I told her to bring her paper and colors to the office with me. She sat quietly, coloring picture after picture, while I worked at the computer. Every five minutes or so, she would say something, and I would reply.

"What color should I make this one?"

"How about red" "Hunh?"

"How about red" "Red?"

"Yes, red"

I would nod my head up and down, never looking away from the computer.

"Okay"

About every 20 minutes, she would want to give me a hug, tell me she loved me and kiss my hand. Then she would go back to her art. When one was finished, she would give it to me, and I'd tack it to the corkboard in the room.

"This looks so peaceful" Tom had sauntered down the hall on his rounds. "Big difference from having the door closed so you could be left alone to do work."

"I know, it just works. I don't know why. I guess she finally trained me." I rolled my eyes, winked at him and went back to my typing.

"When is Thanksgiving?" Janet asked, looking up at me.

"In about 6 weeks." I told her, absentmindedly thinking about how quickly the year had passed.

"Are we going to have Turkey and pie?" she asked.

"Yes, and stuffing and sauce."

"And gravy?"

"Yes, gravy. What do you like best, Janet?"

"I like white meat and red berries and brown pie". Brown pie, I began to think. Brown pie. What brown pie? "Do you mean pumpkin pie?"

"Yes, but it looks brown on the outside."

"Yep, brown pie."

Thanksgiving is a big meal day. One of the seemingly small things anyone keeps as their health and youth disappear is the option of what to eat. And we do a big spread at Thanksgiving and Christmas with lots of choices. We try to put together enough different items to please everyone, at least a little bit. All the staff working that day help serve good food while it is still hot. And then, when all the residents have had seconds if they want them; we employees eat too.

I watch the hands brush through her fine, gray brown hair. The hands then divide her hair down the back of her head and take one side of the hair, brushing it together. The hands wrap a rubber band made for hairstyles around the hair. Small blue beads lock together to keep the hair in place. As I watch the hands divide this hair and start to braid it, I seem to feel my hair being braided. My mother would braid my hair every morning before school. Her hands seemed to move effortlessly while doing my hair. And the hands I watched were moving effortlessly. My hair is shorter now, and it is mostly white gray. Much grayer than the hair being braided now, by hands I'm watching, my hands.

When I finish, Janet hugs me, kisses my hands and takes her brushes back to her room. She is very particular about how she looks. She chooses how she wants her hair done. Today she directed pigtails, like Marie.

"Here's your brush, go put it away in your room". I watched her move her walker around and lean over the front of it while going down the hall.

Children, I don't have children. Wanted some once. But then, the sisters have no family, and I have no children. Or do I? I think about their safety daily. I try to make sure they have choices, but in the back of my mind I know they aren't going to 'learn' more from each experience than they know now. They are so aggravating and demanding of simple things, the same things every day. And they are also very complex. The more I try to stay unattached and professional the more I have to lie to myself that they are only two of the many residents my nursing license cares for. And yet, I know when time comes for them to go somewhere else, or die of old age; I'll have a very large hole in my heart.

I walked down the hall to Marie's room, wanting to give her clean laundry. I knocked twice. No one answered the door, and I slowly opened the door. The sisters were sitting on the side of the bed, in the dark. They sat very close together. At first, they appeared distant, fuzzy to my eyes. But I could clearly see that there was closeness between them I do not have with my sister. For a moment I had the feeling I was interrupting a sacred time, two women so very close, over so many years. I was sorry I had to infringe on their time. At times Marie has seemed to be afraid of her older sister, but right now, they seemed connected by time, place and circumstance.